30p

MY BIRDS by W. H. DAVIES

OTHER BOOKS BY
W. H. DAVIES

MY BIRDS

W. H. DAVIES

LONDON

JONATHAN CAPE 30 BEDFORD SQUARE

FIRST PUBLISHED 1933
REPRINTED APRIL 1933

JONATHAN CAPE LTD., 30 BEDFORD SQUARE, LONDON
AND 91 WELLINGTON STREET WEST, TORONTO

PRINTED IN GREAT BRITAIN BY J. AND J. GRAY, EDINBURGH
PAPER SUPPLIED BY GROSVENOR, CHATER AND CO. LTD.
BOUND BY A. W. BAIN AND CO. LTD.

CONTENTS

MY BIRDS

THE GARDEN

DREAMERS

There was a poet once who died,
His casement opened wide;
With his two hands he clasped his book,
And died with his last look
Fixed on the brightest star –
How great some poets are!
I too have my ambitious end,
With one green leaf in either hand –
And save the small breast-feather
Of a little bird for the other!

I WOULD like to say at the beginning of this book that my knowledge of birds is very limited, and that the inward urge to write it is all a matter of love, and of no scientific value. So that my only excuse is that these birds have so taken possession of my mind that I can find no other relief than by writing a whole book about them. Needless to say, my relief will be only temporary, for even now, as I listen to this Blackbird, I am still in hope that when his short life is over, I, with my longer life, will be here to enjoy the songs of his son or daughter, and perhaps his grandchildren too.

It is certainly a great comfort to sit in one's own garden and listen to the Blackbird's song. To me it seems to be life at its highest value, to which all other kinds of life appear dull, unhealthy, and wasteful. It is wonderful that now, when my own voice begins to fail, that I am able to sit here and listen to my sweeter contemporaries — the Blackbird, Chaffinch, and Thrush. They sing for me without expecting commendation, and I can praise them without jealousy. That birds are the happiest things on earth, there seems to be no doubt; their very movements tell you that, without a study of their songs. And I would not care to believe, in spite of what scientists say, that they do not suffer much grief when they lose each other's company.

On one occasion I saw a parent Thrush feeding her baby on my garden lawn. But the old bird had no sooner left it for a minute, to go in search of food, than a strange cat sprang from under the hedge and claimed its victim. And although I was quickly on the spot, it was too late, for the cat disappeared over the garden wall. Soon after this the old bird re-appeared and ran here and there in search of her lost baby, till I, suffering some pain myself, went out for a walk, to escape the sad sight. When I returned, two hours later, I saw the old bird huddled under the hedge, as motionless as a stone. Time after time I returned to my window, and it was still there, in such a stupor that if the same cat had returned it could have had the mother as easily as it had had her baby. That this bird kept the same huddled position, without moving an inch, for more than half an hour, is quite enough to show how much a bird suffers grief.

We will now consider our garden, for it will be obvious that unless a man maintains a suitable place he will not make a great number of bird friends. Let the house be detached, if possible, set well back from the road, and the garden not less than a quarter of an acre. That will be quite large enough for an ordinary person, though I, with my abnormal love, require much more. This garden, say a quarter of an acre, should contain quite a number of trees without interfering with the light and air that are necessary to the house. It must be remembered that a bird only recognises one thing as a real friend, and that is a green leaf; and all other things are mere acquaintances. Unless these birds have boughs on which to perch, high places in which to sit in safety, how can we expect them to remain and sing, when they have once come? These are the conditions under which they will live near you. We must bear in mind that these birds sing for their own pleasure; and if a garden is green, leafy, and quiet, it does not matter who lives in the house, a poet, a pork-butcher, or both. Having found this house, generously covered with leaves, and several large trees around it, you can then endear it with the pet name of 'Birdland Place,' or 'Corner,' and leave its more matter-of-fact address to be used by shopkeepers and the indifferent world beyond.

'Let there be leaves,' that is my cry, and the birds will surely follow. Do not be daunted if the leaves around your windows should harbour insects that invade your bedroom, but remember that the birds are there every morning to cheer your ears before you have opened your eyes. Explain this little matter to your gentle wife, but never try to persuade a landlady.

I remember on one occasion seeking lodgings in a strange house, and being ordered by the landlady not to open my bedroom windows because of the insects outside, and it was a hot night in August too! But although this woman had a strong dislike to garden insects, it did not take me long to find out that she had no objection to fleas! My body could soon bear witness to that.

At the extreme end of my orchard, in one corner, stand two large ash trees, two fir trees, and a quantity of undergrowth, making a dense mass of leaves. It is so quiet and private that the wildest birds come there, the Owl, the Magpie, and the Rook. But to-day I have been led to understand that another strange creature visits the spot, and I am now waiting to meet him face to face. A friend of mine has picked up a cone and, after examining it, said, 'You have a Squirrel coming to your garden, and here are the marks of his teeth.'

But no garden, unless it contains a pond tucked away in a far corner, can be called a perfect place. If a garden is not jewelled in one hole, it is still without its greatest charm. Not that I would have a stream running through it, however much I like the idea of water. My water must be still, looking up to Heaven with a quiet adoring eye, even as I do myself. It must not gallop wildly in times of flood, and throw mud in the eyes of encroaching flowers. I will have no active water anywhere in my garden. There shall be no marble Cupid on my lawn – unless he lies on his back and has so strong a water-force that he can throw it higher than a tree and piddle on fifty square yards of grass. But this pond, up to the present, is only a dream that waits fulfilment.

In my room last night I looked towards my Porcelain Man, where he stood on a shelf against my wall. It did not take me long to see that he cast a strong rich shadow behind him, clean-cut and bold. To my surprise I saw that his shadow was so bold and strong that even it could cast a shadow too. And there I sat astonished, fascinated by a shadow's shadow, for the first time in my life. So that when my Porcelain Man fails to hold my attention, and his beautiful shadow has not sufficient force to impress me, the shadow itself casts a distinct shadow too – almost too thin to see – and I am lost in wonder. All this belongs to the world of shadows and dreams, but they are the only things worth having, and never to be called a waste of time.

The necessity of having a pond or pool in my garden has now come in full force, and all since yesterday. I have had cause to visit a large city, some thirty miles from home, and what I saw on the journey has made a strong impression on my mind. No doubt I saw thousands of people during the day, and yet I can only remember seeing one man. We were passing through a green stretch of country at the time, that had neither house nor building of any kind. And on looking out of the window of my coach, I suddenly saw a man fishing, sitting all alone at the far end of a quiet pool. There he sat, smoking his pipe, with his fishing-rod between his legs; not so far away but what I could see the happy smile on his face – a smile that seemed to have spread all over his bald head, which lay bare and open to the sun. That man, sitting there happy and alone, detached from all his kind, seemed to me to be the one immortal of his day, and equal to the gods that rule our destiny. Of all the thousands I had seen during my journey, he was the only one I can remember – the one man on earth to equal the one Sun in Heaven. It was worth going a thousand miles to see, and to weep for the folly of us all, when we do not know which way to turn or what to do to find a contented mind.

But if I had this pool in my garden, it would not be a place for fishing – I would only sit there quietly and dream. The fishes could lay their silver bellies on the smooth stones, or heave the weeds on their golden backs; and what I saw I might tell, but no harm would come to them from that.

A pool in my garden would also bring more birds, because of the greater number of insects; and the more birds I have in my garden the more I enjoy life.

One bright morning, when I opened my front door, carrying in my hand the birds' breakfast, there was such a number of them waiting that when they flew up suddenly, as one, the quick transition from light to darkness almost blinded me, and I had to wait for the air to clear before I could step forward. The sound of their wings, when rising, was like a sudden clap of thunder and, for a second or two, I was affected in both my ears and my eyes.

CHAPTER II

BIRDS OF THE PAST

WILD CREATURES

They say wild creatures hide themselves,
　　And seek a quiet place to die:
Would that my end were such as theirs,
　　So strange, so wild a thing am I.

Let no man sneer at me, and say –
　　'We know this poet hides with care;
Inside the Abbey's sacred walls
　　He hides himself – if anywhere.'

I, who have lived for Nature's love,
　　Think nothing of your sculptured stones –
Who sees a dingle lined with moss,
　　And one small row of clean, white bones?

BEFORE I settle down in my garden, I would
like to introduce my readers to three strange
birds that belonged to my earlier life. Two
of these were Parrots, and city birds, while

the other was my sole companion for a whole night in an American forest.

One of these birds was a large green Parrot, called by the usual name of Polly. A sailor on active service had sold this bird to Sailor Tom, who was now settled on shore. The bird had been taught to swear, and Sailor Tom – who was a good swearer too – could enjoy this language with a clear conscience, seeing that it was not he who had taught the bird to use such vile words. In fact, it was because of this clear conscience that Polly learnt to swear more than ever. For if Sailor Tom had not employed such bad language in reviling the late owner for his bad teaching, the bird would have soon forgotten her lessons. So when Sailor Tom said, 'Who taught you that wicked word? The bloody swine!' the bird naturally shouted back, 'The bloody swine.' And when Sailor Tom called the man 'a son of a devil,' Polly joined in with enthusiasm, and screamed in a loud voice, 'The son of a devil!' And every time this happened the old sailor was amazed to think

24

that the bird remembered so much of her past teaching; and without the least idea that it was he, and he only, that was responsible for her good memory.

In the course of time the old sailor married a widow, who had an only child called Emma. The Parrot only lived about four months after this change. But even in that short time it was obvious that the bird had transferred her affection to young Emma. Strange to say, the parrot never used bad language to this child, although she still used it to her master. There was something of a mystery in this, and Sailor Tom spent many an hour on its solution, but all in vain. His idea had always been that his Parrot would be no respecter of persons, but he was entirely wrong. Perhaps there was not much of a mystery after all. For instance, every time Sailor Tom addressed his Parrot, he began with 'Hullo!' Now it happened that the Parrot had been taught in her early days that certain words must follow, and the only thing to say, after hearing this particular word, was 'You bloody swine.' So whenever the Parrot heard this word, it at once gave the full and complete sentence, which was, 'Hullo, you bloody swine!' This rule applied to other words in the same way. The old sailor only had to turn to his Parrot and say, 'Buck up,' and the bird would immediately complete the sentence, as it had been taught, by shouting, 'Buck up, damn you!' It will be quite clear from this that the only reason why the bird did not use bad language to the child was because young Emma always began to address it as 'Polly,' and never once said 'Hullo' or 'Buck up.'

Another form of address employed by the old sailor was to cry, 'Ship, ahoy!' which was always followed by the Parrot shouting, 'Ship ahoy, you damn rotter!' It will be gathered from this that if Sailor Tom had stopped saying 'Hullo,' 'Buck up,' or 'Ship ahoy' – the bird's language would have been as pure as when addressed by young Emma.

The Parrot died swearing, as it had lived.

One morning young Emma thought the bird was acting strangely, and began to address it in her usual way, saying, 'Polly, Polly; Polly's a beauty; Pretty Polly.' The bird repeated these words, but in so feeble a voice that the child called for her stepfather. The old sailor looked at the bird and, seeing that something was wrong, cried in a sharp, cheerful voice, 'Buck up!' The bird no sooner heard this than she shook her feathers, tottered with the exertion, and answered in a shrill voice, 'Buck up, damn you!' These were her last words, for in less than five minutes after this, she was lying dead at the bottom of her cage. But even then, in spite of his great sorrow in losing his Parrot, which had been his companion for a number of lonely years, the old sailor still wished the poor thing had not died swearing; and still could not understand why she swore every time he spoke to her. And it never once occurred to him that had the bird died in the presence of young Emma only, and had not heard the words 'Buck up,' she would

27

never have spent the last moments of her life in blasphemy.

The second bird on my list was also a Parrot, and to be found in the back room of a London tavern. The owner of this bird, and the landlord of this tavern, was not nearly so innocent as old Sailor Tom. For the words he taught this bird were not meant so much to cause amusement as to put money into his own pocket, by causing customers to come often, and to spend more than they could well afford. But the most extraordinary thing about this bird was that he never indulged in strong healthy swearing, but used a language that was sly and suggestive, with a meaning that was unmistakable. It was a cock bird, and to a blind man the voice could easily be mistaken for the voice of a human being. Needless to say, this tavern, and this particular room, was much frequented by a certain class of customer, the woman of the World. For it was here, thanks to the tuition of a crafty landlord, that love-making was made easy. All a woman had to do was to take a seat near a strange man, and leave the result to a bird's language.

The bird did not have a very great number of sayings, but such as they were, they were always clear and to the point. One sentence was, 'Have a drink, my dear.' Another, 'What a nice man!' or 'What a pretty girl!' Another cry was, 'Kiss me, Charlie,' followed by the sound of kissing. The result of all this was that laughter at the bird's sayings was an easy introduction to love-making; removing the shyness from men, and making it more easy for these women to approach them. Sometimes the bird would look straight into a woman's face and ask the question, 'Are you looking for a lover?' At another time he would address his remarks to the man, saying, 'There she is, cuddle the hussy!' This plain, simple language, coming so clearly from the throat of a bird, was startling. The only mistake he seemed to make was that occasionally he looked at the man when he was addressing the woman, and turned to the woman when his words were meant for the man. It need hardly be explained that many a man and woman who met in this room for the first time in their life were not there long before they were sitting dangerously close to each other, and could only find relief at last by leaving arm-in-arm, to find a more private place.

The landlord of this tavern, who was the cause of all this intrigue, and who had taught his bird so well, never seemed to notice what was going on; and never once appeared to notice the bird's remarks, no matter how much laughter they caused. All he did was to come and go, in answer to a bell, and serve drinks to his customers.

A certain number of loose women frequented this tavern night after night, for they knew how easy it was to catch any strange man who came there for a drink. They left the whole matter to a bird, as far as language was concerned, and only made use of looks, which were quite enough. The bird used his tongue in their favour, and bred familiarity in a very short time.

We will now come to my third bird, which belongs to an earlier day. Some years ago, I slept alone at a forest fire, and was kept awake all night by the nagging of an angry bird that objected to my flames and sparks. It is an experience I shall never forget, because of the loneliness of the place, and the loneliness of a wandering life. A night like that, coming at the present time, would probably affect my mental balance. But at that time I was young, strong, and healthy, and had every hope in the future. As I have written a poem about this experience, I will print it here. It can be described better in verse than in prose, as all our greatest moments can.

AYE

How many years since I, a wandering man,
    Sat at a forest fire, for warmth and light!
With but one mate, a bird unseen, and strange
    That kept on crying, all the livelong night –
'Aye! . . . Aye! . . . Aye!'

Though times are changed, and different
    fires are mine,
  Yet if that strange, wild bird could but
    restore
The youth I lost when in his forest glade –
  Would I not come again in rags, and poor?
'Aye . . . Aye . . . Aye.'

COURTING

MAGPIES

I have an orchard near my house,
　Where poppies spread and corn has grown;
It is a holy place for weeds,
　Where seeds stay on and flower, till blown.
Into this orchard, wild and quiet,
　The Magpie comes, the Owl and Rook:
To see one Magpie is not well,
　But seeing two brings all good luck.
If Magpies think the same, and say,
　'Two humans bring good luck, not one' –
How they must cheer us, Love, together,
　And tremble when I come alone!

In beginning this chapter, I am thinking of
a certain courtship that began some ten years
ago, between a girl of twenty-two and a man
who was older. These two lovers met as
complete strangers, knowing nothing of each

other's life or its connections; but as they both had simple natures, they became great friends immediately. As it did not take them long to discover that they both had a strong liking for nuts and fruit, they made arrangements accordingly, and met for the purpose of eating almonds, English walnuts, or cobs. The girl appeared to prefer almonds, or the small, Spanish, black nuts, for the reason that these particular nuts often contained double kernels, which seemed to have a great interest for her especially. For every time he or she had two kernels in one shell it became their strict religion to share them, which the girl had been the first to suggest. But that was not all, for every time this happened both the man and girl must wish for something in secret, and never give the least hint of what it was. The man, who was not rich, usually wished for money and independence, just enough to give him leisure to worship the sun and stars, and to sit until a Blackbird had finished his song.

So much for the man – but what of the

girl? It was quite clear that when the twin kernels arrived suddenly and often, and the man received his share, that he was getting troubled in his wishes, and could not go on thinking of money and nothing else. But every time the girl received hers, she appeared to be more happy and self-possessed – did she save herself from worry by only having one wish?

In the course of time these two lovers married, but they still carried on the old game of eating almonds and sharing twin kernels. One night, when they had been married five years, and she had received one for her share, she began to laugh, and said, 'I have a confession to make, but, when you hear it, you will only laugh at me.' The husband protested that he would not laugh, and would take her confession quite seriously.

'Well, here it is,' she said at last, still hesitating. 'Do you remember the first time we did this – how we shared our almonds every time there were twin kernels, and how we wished for something in secret? Let me now confess that I wished and wished the same thing every time. I wished that you were my husband; I wished it until it became true.'

This married couple still share their nuts, when they get twin kernels. I know this for certain, on my own life and the life of the woman who shares it. But when we share our kernels now, there is no difference in our wishes; we only have one wish between us, which is to live on in the same happy way, side by side and close together, even as two kernels in one shell.

In thinking of the above, I have been reminded of the sweetest and most attractive form of courtship that has come to my knowledge. It was between a country boy and a country girl, and happened at the back door of a country house. The boy, who delivered goods at the back door, had taken a strong liking to the maid, but did not know how to overcome a cold form of civility. But one fine morning, when he was waiting for her to answer the door, he happened to see a big black Crow perching on a tall tree near the house. This was his chance, and, in spite of the colour coming and going in his face, and a heart that beat faster, he made up his mind to take advantage of this and speak his mind. So that when he had delivered his goods, and before the maid could shut her door, he pointed to the Crow, and said –

'One Crow – sorrow,
  Two Crows – joy;
Three Crows – a letter,
  Four Crows – a boy;
Five Crows – silver,
  Six Crows – gold;
Seven Crows – a secret
  That has never been told.'

Having said this he left in haste, but he had given the maid plenty to think about. He had done his part and made a beginning, and the question now is – how will she behave? If she has a kind smile and an encouraging look, when he comes next time, he will muster his courage and invite her to walk out with him, or go to the Fair. But if she is cold, indifferent, and collected, he will know then that the charm has not worked in his favour, and the seeing of one Crow has brought him bad luck. He will think of his folly in drawing her attention to one black Crow, which means sorrow; and regret that he did not wait to see two Crows together, before he began love-making, knowing that two Crows mean joy.

It was certainly a handsome invitation to love, and deserves a lot of kind consideration. But probably the maid has heard it before, from other lovers, and it is not new enough to excite her curiosity. However, there was one good and faultless reason why it was never encouraged, which was that the girl already had a lover, and it only needed the finding of a convenient cottage to make her a married woman.

In the country there seems to be a great number of superstitions that relate to birds. It will be seen from the poem at the beginning of this chapter that to see one Magpie brings bad luck, and to see one Crow means sorrow. But the strange part is this, that, when we see one Crow, we do nothing to charm the ill that we expect to follow; whereas, when we see one Magpie, we immediately raise our hats in the belief that that is a sure remedy against misfortune.

On one occasion I was out walking with a staid old man, who had more common sense than education, and was not without a certain amount of wit and humour. As we walked along he suddenly raised his hat, to my surprise, for I did not see any lady near, or even in the distance. However, to be on the safe side, I quickly followed his example, out of respect to the man's acquaintances. But as soon as I was certain that we had the whole road to ourselves, without any other human being in sight, I questioned him about his movement.

'Did you not see that Magpie?' he asked seriously. 'This is not the first time to-day that I have had to raise my hat to a Magpie to save myself from misfortune. But as you did not see the bird yourself, there was no cause for you to follow my example.'

Now this old man was of such an independent character that, although he raised his hat to a strange bird, I am not sure that he would have done that if a queen had passed in her coach, and the king was with her, still wearing his crown.

Another superstition, which is quite common in the country, is that when a Robin taps at the window, or crosses the threshold, bad luck will surely follow. But the experience of a lady friend seems to have been the reverse; for when a pretty Robin became friendly enough to enter her porch, it seems to have brought good luck to the both of of them. What she did was to go back to the kitchen and fill a bowl with warm water, which she placed before her small visitor. To her surprise the Robin accepted a tepid bath at once, and enjoyed himself immensely. In fact, he enjoyed it so much that he came back morning after morning to enjoy the luxury of a warm bath. I don't believe any-

one had ever done this before, and that no
other Robin had ever known such an experience. There was not much bad luck in
this, either for the woman or her little bird
friend, for both of them enjoyed a number of
happy mornings together. So that if a Robin
ever enters your house in winter, offer him
a bowl of warm water. Let him taste it first,
and then see him stand thoughtfully on the
rim, before he takes his first tepid bath, and
makes up his mind to come again.

CHAPTER IV

BIRD-NESTING

A DOG'S GRAVE

My dog lies dead and buried here,
  My little Pet for five sweet years.
As I stand here, beside her grave,
  With eyes gone dim, and blind with tears –
I see it rising up and down,
As though she lay in a sleeping-gown.

Forgive me, Pet, that half these tears,
  Which make my eyes go dim and blind,
Should come from thoughts of love
      betrayed,
  When I had trust in my own kind:
And Christ forgive this living breath
That links such lives with my dog's death!

THE reason why I introduce a dog into this book on Birds is because my dog Betty, a little Sealyham, was a most successful bird-nester. She did not rely on her sharp eyes,

as boys do when they search the hedges for
nests that contain eggs, but relied more on
her quick ears that could hear the young
baby birds, after the eggs had been hatched.
So that every time she passed a hollow tree or
wall and heard the sound of young birds, she
invariably sat up, as in the act of begging, and
waited patiently for my approach. It was
some time before I knew the meaning of this.
She had sat up, time after time, before a
hollow apple tree, until I began to wonder
if the dog worshipped trees, as a man might
worship the sun. Every time she did this,
I stepped forward at once, and only answered
the appeal in her eyes by bringing her away
to another place. But I had not done this
more than three or four times when I heard
the young birds crying inside the tree, and
saw the hole through which the old birds
passed in and out to feed their young.

The sitting up of this little pet dog, and her
patience in doing so until she got what she
wanted, was sometimes a great trouble to me,
because of my sad thoughts. For I used to

picture myself as lying dead and the dog sitting up patiently, begging to be nursed, with no one coming there to relieve her or reward her for her affection. For it must be remembered that this small pet dog spent half its life on my knee, and slept at the foot of my bed. Pages and pages have I written with my book on one knee and my dog on the other, and many a song has taken shape in my brain under the same conditions. It will be understood from this that my dog was a faithful companion, with no other kennel than its master's shadow. I am not a man to grumble much, dissatisfied with life, and forever pointing to a place where I think Nature sins. But I still think Nature sinned in this – that it did not give a dog longer life, considering its importance to those who have few human friends, and thinking of the animal's love, trust, and fidelity.

We will now return to birds, with Betty's success in finding a second nest, which was in a pear tree planted against my garden wall. I had seen her sitting up for a long time in

front of this tree, and came to the conclusion
at once that she had found another nest. So
that when I rejoined her I was not at all
surprised to hear the weak crying of young
birds, coming from half-way up the tree. The
greatest trouble of my life at this time was
that we also had a cat, which is a great trial
to a lover of birds. He was certainly a very
fine cat, jet-black and shiny, and was known
by the name of Pharaoh. That was his
proper name, usually applied to him in the
morning. But at noon, when he purred
lustily as he drank milk, it was not unusual
to call him 'Gussie, the Guzzler.' And at
night, when he lay sleeping in a chair, lazy,
sleek, and fat, it gave me pleasure occasionally
to point a finger of scorn, and say, 'You
Bloated Aristocrat!'

I would like to say here that these two
animals, both cat and dog, worked together
in perfect harmony, and sometimes to my
distress. For instance, I had noticed that a
great number of my apples lay strewn on the
grass, and it was impossible to think that

seemed to be full of parent birds, that flew off with every scrap of food available, to feed their young. So that every time I filled their bread-table, for the pleasure of seeing them at their meals, they did nothing but grab a morsel and fly off with it, to use it elsewhere.

It did not take me long, when I reached my pear tree, and took Betty in my arms, to see that it contained a large nest, which could be either a Blackbird's or a Thrush's. And I did not have long to wait before two Blackbirds came along and entered their nest, carrying some of the bread that I had distributed. But just before these Blackbirds entered their nest, I saw, to my surprise, that two little Blue Tits were leaving. What was the meaning of this? At first I was very much annoyed, for I thought that these two Blue Tits were robbing the young ones of their food, as fast as the parents brought it, and starvation must surely follow. But it did not take me long to find that there was a perfect understanding between these birds, and that the little Blue Tits were actually helping the Blackbirds to feed their young ones, going and coming with as much eagerness as the parent birds themselves. It seems that the Blackbirds had said to the little Blue Tits, 'Now, my dears, you have reared your own family, and have no more responsibility. Will you not come and help us to rear ours?'

The Blue Tits had accepted this invitation, and were now doing all they could to help their bigger friends. And although the Blackbirds brought large mouthfuls of provender, according to their capacity for carrying it, it must not be thought that the little Blue Tits, carrying their more dainty morsels, were not doing very much in the matter. For it is certain that they were in attendance more often, and were often kept waiting on an adjoining branch until the real parents had left their nest and gave their little friends freedom to enter. It was the first time I had ever seen anything like this, and I went to the pear tree day after day, until the young Blackbirds were feathered and grown, and

to be seen outside their nest, waiting for more
courage to fly a little farther away.

Near my house I had a larger pear tree,
which bore fruit in plenty, probably because
its roots were in a drain. The pears were
small, but soft and sweet, and for a time
attracted thousands of Wasps and scores of
Starlings. It was during this period that
Betty was stung, grew sick, and died.

We are but mortal, and we have our sting,
Like Wasps and Bees and many a smaller thing:
Make me a Bee that stings in self-defence,
And not a Wasp that stings to give offence.

On looking through some unpublished
work, I have come across a little poem called
'Dogs,' which was written in my study some
time ago, with Betty in her usual place on
my knee. As this seems a fit place to use it,
here it is.

When I was once a wandering man,
   And walked at midnight, all alone –
A friendly dog, that offered love,
   Was threatened with a stone.

'Go, go,' I said, 'and find a man
   Who has a home to call his own;
Who, with a luckier hand than mine,
   Can find his dog a bone.'

But times are changed, and this pet dog
   Knows nothing of a life that's gone –
Of how a dog that offered love
   Was threatened with a stone.

The trouble in dealing with a subject like this is that the author may appear cheap and sentimental. For a great number of people who keep animals, and are kind to them, are not greatly concerned at their loss. They get other animals to take their place, much the same as they buy new clothes to replace the old. But for myself, I am so fond of dogs that I do not care to keep one, for fear of losing it, and the great difficulty in giving it the attention it asks for, and so well deserves. So I am very much afraid that Betty is the last, as far as I am concerned.

Pharaoh, now old and blind in one eye, is still with us, preserving the most silky, the most glossy black skin in the whole world. It is always soft and warm, even in winter; and when he is sleeping I often warm my cold hands on his back. I have just seen him lying fast asleep on a high chair. Lord, if he only knew that a mouse was even now sitting up under that very chair, and in the act of rubbing its own innocent little face! This I have just seen, and left quietly, not wishing to disturb either of them.

When this pet dog was buried, the only flower on her grave was one small violet. But when it is remembered that I never pick flowers, and this was the last and only violet in the whole garden – when this is remembered, it will be understood that the cause must have been strong and the sacrifice great. That one flower was important in simplicity, and richer than any wreath. It was the gift of a child.

CHAPTER V

BIRDS IN TROUBLE

ON FINDING A DEAD BIRD UNDER MY WINDOW

Here you lie, with feathers cold and wet –
To dig a grave for you will cause no sweat!
I never felt your body warm with blood,
And now I hold you longer than I should.
What does it matter, if we live or die –
You with a cherry-tempted heart, or I?
The sun in Heaven has his own heat and glow,
And, when all flesh is gone, the grass will
     grow.
Yet still I hope that you have left a son
Or daughter here, to do what you have done –
To tap my window sharply, without warning,
And be the first to wish a friend 'Good
     Morning.'

Considering the number of birds one sees
in a well-wooded garden, it is surprising how
seldom we find one dead. But on going into

53

my garden this morning I have had this unpleasant experience, and find the morning not as bright as it looks. I have had to dig a grave for this small corpse and bury it, before the insects light on its eyes, or the bigger things ruffle its cold feathers. I have been able to handle it tenderly with my bare hands, before anything has come along to mar its beauty. It was a very small corpse, and not heavy; it was so light and small that my only spade was a penknife, and I only had to lift a few spoonfuls of earth.

It is not often that a dead bird is found in a garden, unless the place has telephone or other wires running across it, and the birds strike them in their flight. The country roads are, of course, much more dangerous for birds, for in addition to telegraph wires, which on main roads are sometimes hung thickly from pole to pole – in addition to these, the birds are also in danger of being struck by a fast motor car, and it is not often that they recover from their injuries. But what I have found in my garden, on several occasions, is a stunned bird, that had struck its head either against a bough or my wall or window. In cases of this kind I always went to the rescue at once; not because the bird would not recover in due course, but because it was at the mercy of cats. Even my own cat Pharaoh, with his one eye, would have been a serious danger then, and would have soon made the bird's recovery an impossibility. So that every time I heard a thud at my window, and had my eyes elsewhere, I always knew the cause, and lost no time in going out of doors. When I had done this, on one occasion I found a fine big Blackbird, standing under my window in a dazed condition. He was so dazed that I was able to pick him up and examine him without awakening his fears. My first thought was to get him a drink of water, but a second thought suggested brandy. In thinking of these two drinks I still had serious cause to think of a third. For it was now necessary to get hold of my cat and give him some milk, so that he would not resent being shut up in the kitchen until the Blackbird was well recovered and away. Although I did not know much about birds, except that I had a life-interest in their songs and movements, yet, for all that, I knew that this bird, being still standing upright, was in no great danger; and that as long as he kept an erect position, and did not incline to lie on his side, he would recover, and not die.

Now I do not know whether this Blackbird was not so ill as I had supposed, and was on the point of recovering, or whether it was the quick effect of a sip of brandy; whatever it was, it was quite certain that the bird not only took new life immediately, but it also showed a strong fighting spirit and pecked at my hand furiously. In fact, he seemed to say, after one little sip of brandy, 'Bring your damn cat here now, and see what I'll do with him!' The next moment he flew off, still swearing loudly, as though I had taken advantage of his temporary stupor and tried to steal his golden bill.

In my last chapter I told you how two

little Blue Tits helped their bigger friends
the Blackbirds in the rearing of their family.
It is now my firm belief that it is quite
common for birds to assist each other, even
when of a different feather. For instance,
when a young bird has gone astray, I believe
that other birds help the parents to find it.
I believe, in fact, that there is an organised
search for it, in the same way as the whole
population of a mountain town go out in
search of a lost child. There have been
several occasions when I have had cause to
believe this, for I have been present at the
reunion, when a bird has rejoined his companions after having been lost for a time.
So that whenever I have rescued a very young
bird, before the cat has done much harm,
and placed it in safety, I am always confident
of it being found by the parent birds, whether
it is in a tree or concealed in the deep grass.
I remember on one occasion taking a young
Sparrow to my study, after the cat had had
it, to give it food and drink, and to restore
its confidence. It was quite obvious that a

great number of Sparrows knew of this, for they all gathered together on a tree before my window, and waited. After I had kept this young Sparrow for about an hour, and had come to the conclusion that it was fit to be set at liberty, I opened my window and saw him depart. Without loss of time he rejoined his companions, where they still stood waiting. It was then that I heard the great fuss that they all made, knowing that their little friend had been lost and was now found; and knowing that he deserved the welcome of one that was once thought dead and had miraculously come to life again.

There was also another occasion, when I had borne witness to the strong exultation of birds that had parted for a time and had come together again. In my scullery an old stove had been removed, and the opening under the chimney had been blocked up with a thick layer of cement. One day, when I was passing through this room, I distinctly heard a sharp tapping behind the cement, and under the chimney. For one moment I

thought it might have been a rat, and
decided that it would soon go by the same
passage that had brought it there. It was not
until the next day that I had cause to enter
that room again; but when I did so I heard
to my surprise the same tapping as before,
and at once came to the conclusion that it
must come from a bird that had fallen down
the chimney. The job of blocking my fire-
place had cost me a couple of pounds, but I
had no hesitation in getting a strong iron
bar and breaking the cement to rescue a
bird that was there and would die from slow
starvation. It was not long before this was
done and, getting a small hand torch, I threw
its light into the far corner, and there saw a
fine big black bird with shining feathers,
which I at once recognised as a Rook. But
the bird would not come forward, and I had
to coax it with bread and with water, until it
came near enough to the hole to enable it to
see the open door beyond, and to feel the
fresh air that was coming through. So I went
out into the garden, and waited the result,

and by and by the Rook flew out suddenly. If I had not seen him, I would have known this, for there, in a tree close to my house, were three other Rooks waiting; and they no sooner saw the approach of my late prisoner than they set up a strong wild chorus of 'Caw, Caw,' to welcome him back. Had these three birds been his companions when he had lost his balance and fallen down my chimney? Had he been pushed down my chimney by another Rook, who had started to fight him; or had they only been playing a game of 'Around and Around We go,' and one Rook had missed his footing and fallen over the most dangerous edge of a precipice? No matter, what is more interesting to know is this: that his companions, all lovable fellows, remembered what had happened and had waited and waited on a tree-top for over twenty-four hours in hope of seeing their friend again.

And when he did come there was such a clamour of joy from those four throats that if it had lasted much longer I would have had to retire into the house with a sick headache. This lasted for about five minutes, until the whole lot of them left my orchard suddenly, flying off to some place unknown, probably to tell their story to distant relations or friends. But I could still hear them 'Cawing,' loudly and often, until they became specks in the distance, thinking it a joy to be alive, and another trouble past and over.

CHAPTER VI

FEEDING THE BIRDS

CRUMBS AND GUINEAS

How many plates of crumbs, my little friend,
　　Have I now scattered twice and thrice a day?
Have I not crushed a ton or more of bread,
　　In payment for your pretty songs and play?

'When you have said what you have done
　　for us,'
　　A saucy Sparrow answered, speaking bold –
'Then tell the World what we have done for
　　you,
　　Whose well-invested bread has brought you
　　gold:
Give us our daily bread – not worth a penny –
And make a song of it, to charge a guinea!'

In my garden I have a bird-table, made by
my own hands, to attract all except the wilder
kind of birds, which are usually the biggest.
I had secured a flat board, about eighteen

inches square, and made a hole in the middle of it. Through this hole I had forced a stake, until it topped the board by six or seven inches, and had then driven the stake into the earth. I had made a rim all around the table, on which the birds could stand and eat like our Christian selves, when we sit in chairs. The Robins, Tits, Linnets, and Finches made great use of this rim; and only the more greedy birds, such as Starlings and Sparrows, hopped all over my table with a lack of good manners. The table was placed in a certain position near my dining-room window, so that when I was at my own meals I could enjoy the sight of seeing my bird-friends enjoying theirs. As will be expected, this bird-table, being an innovation in my garden, and so near the house, was not an immediate success. With the exception of one Robin, who had always followed me everywhere in the garden, and had often waited for me outside the house – with the exception of this bird, not one patron arrived, and it troubled me to know the reason why. Here was I, a

millionaire in crumbs of bread, though poor
enough in golden pounds, and only one bird
to take advantage of my bounty! However,
this only lasted a few hours, for on the
following day the crumbs disappeared twice
as fast as I could make them. It took me
longer to crush a piece of bread and reduce it
to crumbs than it took the birds to eat them.

As I have said, the patrons of my table
consisted mainly of Sparrows, Tits, and
Finches, with a Blackbird or Thrush occasionally. My usual patrons, among the bigger
birds, were always Starlings. Not that these
birds are tamer than others, but because of
their appetite and greed, which takes them
everywhere. Of all the smaller birds, the
little Wren was the most independent, and
preferred to find her own food. And yet this
tiny creature was often to be seen close to
the house, running under the hedge or
through it, and searching the cracks in my
garden wall. However, I have never blamed
this little creature for any unfriendliness to
man, but rather think, where it concerns

other birds, that it prefers a lonely life and has a dislike to communities; and for that reason it would not eat at the same table as Sparrows and others. It so often prefers using its legs for running, instead of its wings for flying, that I sometimes think it must be half a mouse and half a bird, and wonder which life it favours most. For myself, I favour the mouse part, and only favour her as a bird when she sings.

Some birds can be fed without much trouble, but with others it becomes a difficult matter. For instance, in times of extreme frost, the Blackbirds and Thrushes suffer severely, for the reason that they will not eat bread unless they are at their wit's end to find worms, that cannot be extracted from the hard earth. That is the reason why we must not take the advice of professional gardeners, when they tell us that rotten apples must now be gathered together and burnt as refuse, so as to make a garden look clean and tidy. Nothing of the kind must be done, for these rotten apples, of which Blackbirds are so fond, will help them considerably to go through a hard winter. These birds will do the work so thoroughly, that where a hundred apples had once been, there will not even be one pip left, though the winter is but half over. From this it will be understood why I always felt kindly towards my cat and dog, when they wilfully, and in sport, destroyed my best apples, by knocking them down before their time and biting them. For I knew that these same apples would rot, and be food for many a hungry Blackbird, when the earth was hard and cold, and it was difficult to find snails or worms.

A Rook, being a very wild bird, has never been known to visit a house for food, and they usually keep some distance away, even when a garden is quiet and seldom used. But in spite of this I have seen Rooks more than once swoop down into my orchard for food, and fly off with it to a safer place. In fact, these Rooks were quite common in my orchard, and divided themselves among the different trees, as though to guard the whole

place from every quarter. It was not long before I knew that these birds were professional
thieves and lived on stolen food, taken by force
from their weaker and smaller brethren. How
often have I seen this done! How often have
I seen one of these big burly Rooks employ-
ing frightfulness on a Sparrow, or some other
small bird that has secured a large piece of
bread that is too heavy to carry. The Sparrow
gets hold of this titbit and carries it off to the
orchard, to enjoy it at leisure. But a Rook,
who is on the look-out, seeing this Sparrow
flying with difficulty, because of the weight of
his prize, begins to make a terrible noise with
his voice, and also to make short, sudden, and
quick swoops, until the Sparrow at last is
frightened and drops his prize. And this is
no sooner done than the Rook swoops down
immediately and takes possession, leaving the
Sparrow surprised at what has happened. In
a few minutes the Sparrow returns to the
house, in the hope of finding more bread.
But if he succeeds, and does the same thing
again, he will find other Rooks watching from

the trees, and waiting to employ the same tactics.

On one occasion, when I was standing in my study window, I saw an excellent example of this, for it looked like a real game of Rugby, played by the birds. To readers who do not understand this great English game, it will be necessary to explain that sometimes the ball is secured by a small man, who must then try to dodge a number of men on the opposing side and place the ball behind two posts. On the occasion of which I speak, one of my Sparrows had secured a rather large piece of bread and, being pestered by other Sparrows, who wanted their share, flew off to the orchard, to have it all to himself. He did not know that four large Rooks had the orchard well guarded, one being on the farthest tree north, another on a tree to the south, another to the east, and still another on the farthest tree west.

It was now that the game began, for these four birds no sooner saw this little Sparrow than they attacked him like big heavy forwards in the human game, from every side, to secure the ball – which was a large piece of bread. But the Sparrow was a determined little fellow, and kept on dodging them one by one, until he had circled the whole orchard, in spite of the Rooks attacking to the front and behind, and also on both sides. However, the struggle came to an end at last, and the little Sparrow dropped his ball of bread, which was caught and carried off by one of the Rooks, almost before it touched the ground.

It will be seen from this that the Rook is an unscrupulous bully, who lives on what he steals from weaker and smaller birds, and has no other thoughts at any time. Nevertheless, the Sparrow, having plenty of courage and impudence, is not likely to starve, while the world has houses, pig-sties, stables, and chicken runs. All these are at his disposal.

VOICES OF SCORN

When I had thought my end was near,
   And I must soon prepare to die –
'Be quick! Be quick!' the Mavis called,
   And 'Haw, Haw, Haw!' the Rooks did cry.

MY BIRDS

What bird, with even greater scorn,
    Has come so quickly following after?
Is this the Chaffinch – how his voice
    Reproves me with its wholesome
        laughter!

CHAPTER VII

SAUCY SPARROWS

ONE POET VISITS ANOTHER

His car was worth a thousand pounds and more,
A tall and glossy black silk hat he wore;
His clothes were pressed, like pretty leaves, when they
Are found in Bibles closed for many a day ;
Until the birds I love dropped something that –
    As white as milk, but thick as any cream –
Went pit, pit, pat! Right on his lovely hat!

*   *   *

Lead this unhappy poet to his car –
    Where is his longing now, where his desire?
When left alone, I'll ride him to his grave,
    On my own little horse of wind and fire.

THE above lines will explain themselves, and
I do not wish to add any more particulars, to
give the impression that I gloated over the
whole event. This poet had come from the

city, dressed to attend a function, and had called at my house on the way, to remind me that he also was a poet. A poet of this kind is always in the limelight, and is not often of much consequence. If we tell little children that they must be seen and not heard, shall we not tell poets that they must be heard and not seen? But it must not be thought for one moment that I had trained my birds to treat visitors with such little respect. They had often done this to me, right on my bare face and head, but I had only laughed at the matter. I did not mind the birds doing this, knowing that it was but an accident; and it was only when human beings tried to do the same thing, metaphorically speaking, that I had thought it advisable to make some kind of a protest.

But on this occasion I can hardly believe it was an accident – I would rather believe that the birds objected to seeing such a large shiny object being brought into a simple country garden. Perhaps it would be kinder to think that these birds could not help themselves; that, seeing so fine a hat for the first time in their lives, so worked on their bowels that they needed no other medicine. Never mind what it was; let it be sufficient to know that a *bad* poet, who could make plenty of money, had called on a *good* poet, who could make little, and had gone away humbled and sad. It was not much comfort for him to know that he had made a stronger impression on a few saucy Sparrows than on the poet he had visited.

To-day my garden has a mystery, which has become something of a shock to my imagination. For I had not only never once seen a rat here, but had never seen the least trace of one, in spite of two keen, inquisitive eyes. I had come to the conclusion that my garden, being the haunt of a large number of stray cats, owing to its size and seclusion, had made the place dangerous for these rodents; that they heard the cats fighting or love-making – and no one knew which – and kept away. It must be remembered that at the end of my orchard there was a meadow which not only made my garden more private, but was also of great convenience to the cats. These cats, on quiet nights, made my garden path their 'Lovers' Lane,' until I was forced through loss of sleep to take stones to my bedroom and pelt them through the open window. This was not always a success, for the stones often fell on the soft earth and made no noise to frighten my tormentors. So I came to the conclusion that the dropping of a tin can would have a better effect, which it certainly did.

The mystery of which I am writing was this: I had found a large rat lying dead in one of my garden paths. The body looked so perfect that it seemed quite obvious that it had not been killed by a cat, neither had it been in a fight with its own kind. It seemed to have died peacefully, and a natural death. It was morning at the time, and my first thought was to dig a hole and bury it. But as I had to go to the extreme end of my garden to find a spade, I thought I would remove the dead rat from my path for the time being, and bury it later in the day, when

I had more time. So I picked it up on two short sticks and laid it under a bush. But certain things happened during the day to keep my thoughts busy, and the next time I thought of this dead rat was on the following morning. So I took my spade and made my way up the garden path. But when I reached the bush and looked under it, I saw nothing! And when I searched the near neighbourhood, there was not the least sign, not even a small bone or the splinter of one; not even a hair to show that a dead rat had been there at all. The complete and absolute disappearance of this large dead rat – bone and hair, tooth and nail – was such a startling discovery that I am not able to forget it. If the body had been found by his fellow rats they would have certainly torn it to pieces and eaten the whole lot. But even then a bone or two, or a little patch of hair, would have remained to show what had happened. I have gone over this matter often, but without being satisfied with the result. It is still a great garden mystery, but perhaps my latest thoughts may come the nearest to solving it. Was the body found by carrion birds, whose beaks had carved it in portions, working around the bones as a butcher carves our meat? And when the portions were ready, did they carry them to another place, to feed their young, or to pick the bones for their own selves? That, it seems to me, can be the only explanation; for in that case the hair would go with the flesh, and the flesh would go with the bone.

As I think a rockery is just as important to a garden as a quiet pond, I have been at considerable pains in making one. Some people make a rockery with anything that comes to hand, small stones without any marks of interest, bricks and clinkers, and even beer bottles. Their idea is that the plants and creepers that are planted there will soon grow all over these objects, and no one will know what lies beneath. But my idea of a rockery is entirely different. The stones I select must have so much beauty of their own that I will only allow the plants to act as curls on their foreheads, or sashes at their sides. I will not allow any creeper to grow all over the face of one of my stones, so that people will at last see a green heap and not a rockery. It must be remembered that I am thinking now of very beautiful old stones, such as I have in my own garden. In fact, these stones are so lovely that a neighbour of mine begged to have two or three for his own garden, for a place of honour at the very entrance to his house. Needless to say, this was not the neighbour who had bordered all his flower-beds with inverted beer bottles! But although I did not admit this man as a good gardener and a lover of beauty, I must say that I liked the idea that he had been a good drinker and did not care who knew it. May his empty beer bottles increase, and his flower-beds spread as fast as he drinks!

I had found, on seeing my garden for the first time, a great heap, where a gardener had been burning rubbish for a long time, and had not taken the trouble to spread it and dig it into the land. This heap was now covered with grass and weeds, and the idea had come to me to clean and make a rockery of it. I had heard that a certain farmer had several loads of stone lying in one of his fields, who would be only too glad to get rid of them, charging me a very reasonable sum. So I had ordered these stones to be delivered, having no idea of their appearance. But when they came I was amazed to see how beautiful they were. To the farmer they were no more than idle stones that served no good purpose in his field, but to me they were great jewels and the joy of a lifetime. They were not only different in size and shape, but also in colour. In fact, each stone had a character of its own, and I would no more allow one of their faces to be covered by a creeping plant than I would wish a pretty girl would wear a veil.

Here is a little poem about *My Rockery*:

Here in my garden I have lovely stones,
   All old and grey, and some with knobs of
     pearl;
Stones with their silver sides, and amber backs,
   With mossy dimples and with horns that curl.

Would that this rockery were my grave
    indeed,
  The monument where lie my buried bones:
Though people – coming here to think of
    me –
  Might well forget, and stay to worship
    stones!

CHAPTER VIII

THE ROBIN

TO PLAY ALONE

A Tom Tit clinging upside down,
　　Needs nothing more to raise his wonder;
A lonely Trout will play until
　　His own deep whirlpool sucks him under.

So when my money all is spent,
　　And all my merry friends are gone –
What little Tom Tit, Trout, or Child,
　　Will teach me how to play alone?

ALTHOUGH the Robin is a lonely bird, yet judging by the occasional jerks of his body, and the proud way in which he surveys his surroundings, it is quite obvious that life is sweet to him, and to his liking. And every time I hear his voice, when he stands alone, singing on a bough, I am reminded of our old friend Robinson Crusoe, with a song of

I am Monarch of all I Survey. How many times have I seen a Tit, Wren, or Robin, playing all alone in my garden, with a self-contained happiness that should belong to us all, and which is the most desirable independence in the whole world.

Why do we prefer a Robin in our garden to any other bird? He certainly has serious faults, and is not only selfish but pugnacious too. For I have seen this bird deliberately squat down in the middle of a feast of crumbs with no other object than to keep other birds away, just for spite. For after he had squatted there for two or three seconds, making himself look like a hunchback, as a lesson of fright — he flew away satisfied, without having taken a single crumb. After which twenty Sparrows or more, who had been sitting on a tree, terror-stricken and demoralised at this bird's ferocious appearance, were allowed to come down for their share. And even when he has gone, it is not certain that he will not swoop down again suddenly for a second display of frightfulness. And it must not be thought that our Robin has no other ambition than to be the master over Sparrows, which are his own weight and size. For I have seen him actually doing all he could to intimidate a Starling, a bird that is not only twice his size, but is also as quick as a Robin in his movements. However, the Starling, being a greedy bird, usually takes no notice of his small challenger, and goes on eating. Occasionally I have seen a Starling accept the Robin's challenge, and stand up for a fight. In a case of this kind the Robin retires, before anything more serious happens.

It seems to me that the Robin likes to think of titbits, and despises the notion of a great feast and a crowd to attend it. He would rather have my personal attention, with one or two crumbs for his special benefit, than be expected to eat with a number of noisy Sparrows and quarrelsome Starlings. Perhaps he has a right to this – we forgive him his faults because he comes closer than any other bird. Whenever he is spoken to by a human friend, he makes a hop, skip, and a jump, and makes a few trills – and no other bird shows so much affection as that.

I would not say that the Robin is a fighting bird, quarrelsome, and a bully, in spite of his family differences, when they fight each other to possess a certain house or plot of land. That he has advantages, such as keen eyes, is quick on his feet and has a stout heart, does not mean that he is eager in offence – but that he is able in self-defence to protect himself. He is really a gentleman, and the only time he loses his good manners and temper is when he sees a number of other birds eating like gluttons. And if he did not show some spirit, when this happens, he would not be able to secure a single stray crumb for himself, much less the one he has selected with his own eye. In fact, the Robin likes his feast to be on view for a time, to go over it with a careful eye before he makes his selection. But he is not allowed to do this owing to the greed of other birds. It will be noticed often that other birds with the same good manners, such as Tits, Linnets, and

Finches, will also leave a feast untouched when they see the gluttony of others. But these birds, not having the Robin's irritable spirit, instead of remaining to protest, would rather hide their feelings and fly away.

But although I would not say that the Robin is a professional fighter and aggressive, I must admit that Nature has given him all the qualities of a fighting bird, and that he is well able to look after his own life and interests. His erect body, his nimble foot-work in retreat and advance, and his indomitable spirit, are enough to frighten any bird that has not an overwhelming advantage in weight and size.

Only once in all my life have I read anything by Anon. and been disappointed. It was when I read his immortal poem called *Who Killed Cock Robin?* This poem is so full of errors, where poetry makes no attempt to reconcile itself to truth, that I have come to the conclusion that it was a Saturday night's effusion, when the master was the worse for drink. Take this verse, for instance:

Who'll dig his grave?
I, said the Owl,
With my spade and shovel –
I'll dig his grave.

What was Anon. thinking of when he
wrote that? He did not seem to know that
the Mole was a professional digger, in the
same way as our human navvy; and it was
the Mole, and not the Owl, who never digs,
that should have volunteered to have 'dug
the hole.' And, by the way, speaking of
moles and navvies, is it not strange that a
navvy, in spite of being a human mole, still
prefers corduroy to moleskin trousers?

When we come to the second verse we are
more amazed than ever. This is what we read:

Who saw him die?
I, said the Fly,
With my little eye –
I saw him die.

Now who can forgive this Fly for his artful
insinuation that he is only a tiny little creature
with but one eye! Does he think to win our

pity by this and save himself from our ill will, so that he may be allowed his freedom to sport in our sugar-basin, to climb a mutton hill-side, and to gild his wings in golden syrup? Science has told us that a fly has a thousand eyes; and even if he were blind in two or three hundred of them it would make very little difference to his busy life. May we suggest an alteration, as follows:

> Who saw him die?
> I, said the Fly,
> With *every* little eye –
> I saw him die.

The first verse fills us with something like indignation, for this is what we read:

> Who killed Cock Robin?
> I, said the Sparrow,
> With my bow and arrow –
> I killed Cock Robin.

Now this is a very serious mistake, very serious indeed. For who ever heard of a Robin being killed by a Sparrow! The

Robin is, for his weight and size, the greatest
little fighter that ever broke bread or breathed
the breath of life; and if he was killed at all
it must have been by another Cock Robin,
but a Sparrow – never! Throw out your
crumbs, and see how a Robin commands the
feast, in spite of a hundred Sparrows. Perhaps this is not the time of year, with Christ-
mas close at hand, to praise Cock Robin as
a fighter, seeing that he is the one and only
bird we associate with this season of peace
and good will. But Cock Robin was not killed
by a Sparrow! And yet, if we try to reconcile
poetry to truth, it is quite likely that we will
destroy the poetry altogether. For instance,
this would be impossible:

> Who killed Cock Robin?
> I, said the Gudgeon,
> With my little bludgeon –
> I killed Cock Robin.

No, we cannot have Cock Robin blud-
geoned – he must have a more noble end
than that. But whatever happens, Cock

Robin was not killed by a Sparrow! If I should ever have the misfortune to find a dead Robin in my garden, I could have no other thoughts but that he had been killed by a rival and, most likely, a close relation. And I would feel sure that the contest had been so fierce, terrific, and lasting, that no Sparrow would have had the courage to witness it, and would have even flown beyond hearing. How often have I seen a Robin show fight to a Sparrow – but have I ever seen a Sparrow show the least sign of resistance? And when a Robin is foolish enough to challenge a much bigger bird, such as a Blackbird, Thrush, or Starling, he is so quick in retreat that none of these birds can get near enough to punish him, and he has never been known to lose his balance and fall.

On one occasion a great friend of mine, who disliked beetles and feared cows and spiders, drew my attention to a large black-beetle under the kitchen table, and asked me to remove it. With my usual objection to taking the life of anything, I took a piece of paper and lifted it gently on to a shovel, with the intention of carrying it into my garden. For if I had shovelled it up roughly, in the same way as we shovel coal, I might have broken one of its limbs. Now, I think I have already mentioned my Robin, my favourite, who was always in close attendance. This bird was usually to be found at my front door, and followed me all around the garden wherever I went. So when I threw this beetle on a flower-bed in front of the house, I was amazed to see a small bird appear suddenly, pouncing on to the beetle and carrying it away. I was very sorry to see this, after all my care. I had of course forgotten my Robin, otherwise I would have taken the beetle to another door.

When I mentioned this to a friend of mine, who had a great knowledge of birds, it filled her with surprise. She had never known, she said, of a Robin feeding on such a large insect; and wondered if, when he had examined his prize, he had not blamed himself for a foolish mistake, and left the beetle with his hard armour unpierced. But although I have searched my garden for hours, hoping to find a live domestic black-beetle, it has all been without success. So in spite of the doubts of naturalists and bird lovers, I am very much afraid that my Robin swallowed the black-beetle, and made no mistake at all.

CHAPTER IX

A SUMMER'S DAY

FLYING BLOSSOMS

These Butterflies, in twos and threes,
　　That flit about in wind and sun –
See how they add their flowers to flowers,
　　And blossom where a plant has none!

Bring me my hat of yellow straw,
　　To greet them on this summer's morn –
That they may think they see in me
　　Another crop of golden corn!

In my last chapter I dealt with the Robin as
a fighting force of great spirit; a bird that
always seemed to be in perfect training,
active, and never muscle-bound. But to-day
we have had a little quarrel, and I have had to
dismiss him for the time being. He was just
on the point of catching a lovely butterfly,
when I stepped between them quickly. By

doing this I have not only saved a butterfly's life, but have also saved myself from bearing an unforgiving grudge against my favourite bird.

At the present time my garden is full of flowers, and the bees and butterflies have come in corresponding numbers. I am sitting in front of my house, with a book at my side, and wearing a large, yellow straw hat. It has suddenly occurred to me that the colour of my hat has made these bees and butterflies indifferent to my presence; and that they regard me, sitting there so still and quiet, as so much corn, or a certain flower known as golden rod.

Most of the bees are small and brown, and known as honey-bees, where they are now at work filling their bags and thinking of a certain hive. But the bee who fascinates me most is a large, black fellow with an amber belt, who leads an independent life as a wanderer. He is much larger than the common bee, and, seeing him there makes me think of a stallion among ponies. He has a much deeper voice than the brown bee, and it comes low and deep, like a voice from the grave. He is so heavy, and so clumsy in making love, that some of the weaker and more slender flowers are bent double on their stalks.

It must not be thought that because the birds have now done singing that the garden is without a sound, for the whole place is full of insects; and the accumulated result of so many of them produces a low murmur that goes on all through the summer's day, from the beating of millions of little wings. But the human ear has to be well trained, otherwise it would not be heard. It is necessary to sit very quiet and still, and to listen intently. If we sit in the garden whistling or humming our own favourite tunes, we will not hear it. We must wait patiently, listening, until we become conscious of a low murmur that goes on and on without a break, even for one second. And if we listen until the sound acts as a lullaby and makes us drowsy, and we sleep for a while – so much the better for our mind and body.

It is not generally known that a Thrush
has a great advantage over every other bird
because of its wonderful sense of hearing,
which is even more remarkable than the
vision of an Eagle or Hawk. The first time
I suspected this, and proved it, I was filled
with astonishment; for I came to the conclusion that if a man had the same sense of
hearing in proportion to his greater size, he
would be able to hear the music of the spheres
with his naked ears, and without the help of
any kind of instrument. In fact the Thrush
discovers his food by listening for it, and only
uses his eyes in case of danger. I had watched
one of these birds on my lawn and noticed
that although he hopped from place to place,
after long intervals of standing motionless
and listening intently, yet, for all that, he
never once looked on the ground. This went
on for some time, until suddenly he pounced
on a certain spot and, to my surprise, began
to tug at a worm. So that every time a
Thrush finds a worm that disturbs the earth
but has not yet come to light, it is due to the

bird's wonderful sense of hearing, and without any help from his eyes. Neither the Blackbird nor the Starling has this gift, although they both have qualities in their favour. For instance, the Starling, who is the greediest bird on earth, as I have said before, is not dainty, and can eat almost anything. And the Blackbird's advantage is that he can make a good meal on rotten fruit and wild berries, when his friend the Thrush is finding it extremely difficult to find worms.

My first thought, when I saw a Thrush standing so still and listening, was that the bird was afraid to move because of danger. But when he even came closer to me and began to tug a fat worm out of the earth, I knew at once that he had listened and heard, and was certain that he had made no mistake. He could always trust his ears, and if he hopped away at last without digging at the earth, it was quite certain that no worms had stirred within a foot or two, and he had listened in vain. Unfortunately for the Thrush, when the earth is frozen hard the worms are not able to stir or make the least move, and then the bird suffers from want of food. It is now that the bird-lover must come to the rescue and feed him. For although he prefers snails and worms, he will eat anything in emergency. In the spring he will repay us for our trouble. Even in February, before the Blackbird has tuned his notes, this Thrush will greet us cheerfully with his short Cuckoo-like call of 'Be quick! Be quick!' Wherever we are, and whatever we are doing, we will hear this and be amused. Until, later in the year, he takes the highest little branch that will support his weight, on the very top of a tree, and sing a fuller song, perfect and sweet.

It is so bright this morning that I am surprised at the wonderful effect it has on my mind. For although I love the rain as a walking companion, I find it very depressing when confined to my house and garden, especially when it continues hour after hour and for several days. My mind then gets the effect of being sodden, even as the brown soil at my door.

It is so bright that I am completely taken by surprise, because of the sudden and violent appearance of a night-bird. This is a large Owl who, crying for mercy in a loud voice, has flown across my garden to find shelter and safety in a thick growth of ivy. For he is being attacked by two very small birds that look like Tits, who are determined that such a creature shall not find a place in the sun. It will be remembered that although the Owl sees well enough at night, yet in the sun, and by day, he is almost blind. For that reason he never ventures forth in the day, and keeps in hiding. Now what possessed this silly bird to come forth on such a bright day as this? Was he hiding near the nest of these small birds and did not know it? And did they rout him out, recognising him as an old enemy, and knowing of his blindness? That they had pestered him with their attack, giving him no rest, was quite clear; and it was also clear that he was in fear of his life and let the whole world know it. Not that these small birds could do him any harm, for even the working of his heavy wings would have been enough to have sent them to the earth stunned and perhaps dead. But they managed to escape this danger and continued their attack until he was not only well away, but was no longer a menace or eyesore to such birds as enjoyed the morning light.

When I enjoy a day like this, with all this wonderful light, I feel so grateful and so generous that I could not possibly destroy life – not even the life of a rat or snake.

A BRIGHT DAY

My windows now are giant drops of dew,
   The common stones are dancing in my eyes;
The light is winged, and panting, and the
     world
   Is fluttering with a little fall or rise.

See, while they shoot the sun with singing
     Larks,
   How those broad meadows sparkle and
     rejoice!
Where can the Cuckoo hide in all this light,
   And still remain unseen, and but a voice!

Shall I be mean, when all this light is
    mine?
  Is anything unworthy of its place?
Call for the rat, and let him share my joy,
  And sit beside me here, to wash his
    face.

CHAPTER X

WORMS AND CRUMBS

BREAST TO BREAST

What strange commotion, Love,
  Is seen on yonder bough?
'It's only a bird,' said she –
  'Or little winds that blow.'
Only a bird, my Love?
  Who sees the best –
When bird and leaf together
  Are fluttering breast to breast!

ALTHOUGH I enjoy the Thrush at a distance, when he sings on a bough, I often prefer the Sparrow as a close companion. The reason is this, that the Sparrow feeds on seeds and grain, and is never to be seen in the act of tugging a fat worm out of the earth, which is such a common sight with the Thrush. Even the Starling, with all his bullying greed, is seldom to be seen doing this. The Robin does it often and is forgiven, because we are so delighted to find him right at our feet, and we overlook the fact that he is devouring worms. In fact, when I see a Thrush eating worms, I can never get over a certain squeamishness; and it is this sympathy for the worm that has always prevented me from fishing. This sight always brings to mind a certain man that I knew in the past, an out-of-work glass-blower, who was then in the last stage of consumption. This man had been told that a good feast of snails taken daily, would give him health and strength, and restore his vitality. So every morning he went forth into the country, taking a small quantity of salt with him; and every afternoon he returned satisfied with his success. Seeing that this man took neither pan, pot, nor kettle with him, and always returned without his salt, I soon began to have a horrible suspicion. Thinking to put this suspicion on a truthful basis, I thought I would question him, and at once offered him some tobacco.

'No, thank you,' he said, 'I never smoke.'

This question was, of course, only to lead to another of far more importance.

'Could you oblige me with a match?' I asked, pretending that my own could not be found.

'I am very sorry,' answered the glass-blower, 'but, being a non-smoker, I have not had a match in my possession for several months.'

This proved my suspicion to be correct.

Thinking of this glass-blower always led me to think of another strange man whom I had known in the past. Passing down the Westminster Bridge Road and then bearing to the left, the reader will find himself in a street that leads direct to Hercules Road. It is a poverty-stricken area, and the cry of this later Macedonia is for better houses to live in. If the reader has any knowledge of Literature or the Arts, it will interest him to know that it was in Hercules Road that William Blake lived, and, with his mind like an egg with a double yoke, or a shell with two kernels, devoted his life to his two professions as an artist and as a poet, and mastered them both. But the inhabitants of Ware Street had no knowledge of the finer Arts, and if anyone had inquired as to where Blake the poet had lived, it would be hardly likely that he would have been any the wiser for his question. However, to inquire of William Blake, the cat's-meat man, and not the poet, would have been more successful; for there was not a man, woman, or child in the whole neighbourhood, who did not know where that man had lived. And although he had only lately left it, and would probably never return to it again, it was quite certain that his name would not be forgotten for a good many years to come. In the eyes of the Sanitary Authorities the house where William Blake, the cat's-meat man, had lived was no better and no worse than others; but in the eyes of the inhabitants the house was morally condemned and unfit for habitation. The poverty in this street was proved by the number of children to be seen, for

the poorer the people are the larger are their
families. But none of these children played
in front of that house; and when their
mothers passed down the street, they made
their Sign of the Cross by shivering and
wrapping their shawls more closely around
their shoulders. We will now hear the reason
why.

For some time past the inhabitants of
Ware Street had been puzzled at the mysterious disappearance of their cats. More than
a dozen of these creatures had melted into
the Unknown, without leaving a single hair
to show which way they had gone. Not one
cry of distress had been heard, to lead to any
suspicion of violence; and, seeing that none
of these cats had come home to die, there
could be no question of poison. In fact, dead
cats were as scarce as dead donkeys, either in
the dark corners of back yards or in dust bins.
Day after day people seemed to be searching
for certain cats, which they could not find
dead or alive. After much talk and gossip
among the neighbours, they came to the

conclusion that their pets were being coaxed and enticed into someone's room and then killed; after which their bodies were either buried in the earth or destroyed by fire. But why? That was the question. That cats made a terrible noise at night and were assailed by missiles that never reached their mark, was well known in this neighbourhood; and this human conduct met with the approval of everyone, even to the most devoted lover of cats. We say 'lover of cats,' not the lover of a cat, which is quite different. For a woman's affection for her cat is not worth much if it does not extend to her neighbours' cats; nor can a man truly love his dog if he has no sympathy for other dogs, even though he has no respect for their masters.

One afternoon, Mrs. Higgins, on looking out of her back window on the first floor, saw something that set her thinking, and with some concern too. For she saw her own cat Tim lying on the roof of a neighbour's wash-house, which ran up to the window of a first floor. But what set her thinking more than

ever was to see a man standing in the open
window, trying to coax her Tim to enter.
The cat, it appeared, seemed to be well
pleased at this attention, and after rounding
his back to the shape of a rainbow, began to
walk round in circles, each circle bringing
him nearer to the open window. Stretching
his arm out gently, as soon as the cat was near
enough to touch, the man stroked it nearer
and nearer. Then all at once Mrs. Higgins
saw to her horror that her cat was being lifted
fiercely off the roof, drawn through the open
window, and flung into the room, and the
window shut quickly.

'That room is Tim's coffin,' thought Mrs.
Higgins, 'and when that man closed his
window, he put the lid on!'

In less than fifteen minutes after this
unpleasant experience, Mrs. Higgins was
knocking violently at her neighbour's door.
But the door was not opened immediately,
for the simple reason that Mrs. Berry, the
landlady, had a strong objection to this
display of force; and when people knocked

too loudly, she made them wait. But when Mrs. Higgins knocked again without waiting any reasonable time, and more loudly still, Mrs. Berry became alarmed, thinking that someone had come in the king's name, and must not be kept waiting by a commoner. However, when she had opened the front door and saw no other than her neighbour Mrs. Higgins, her annoyance returned, and all she could do was to stare coldly into her neighbour's face and wait for an explanation.

'I have come for my cat Tim,' began Mrs. Higgins firmly, 'and I am going to take him back home whether he is dead or alive.'

'But Tim is not in this house,' answered Mrs. Berry, in an alarmed voice, to think that her house should ever be suspected of having anything to do with the mysterious disappearance of her neighbours' cats.

'Tim is in the back room on your first floor,' cried Mrs. Higgins emphatically, 'and his abductor is a man who is dressed in black and has a very white face.' If you are a lady, Mrs. Berry, and reasonable, you will give

me one chance – I ask no more – to get at
that man's dirty-ivory looking skin. Who
is this maggotty-looking man that occupies
one of your back rooms?'

'That's one of my lodgers,' answered Mrs.
Berry, 'and his name is William Blake. Come
in, Mrs. Higgins, and we will clear the
matter up by seeing him at once.'

The next minute the two women were
upstairs, and Mrs. Berry knocked sharply at
a certain door. But it was so long before the
door was opened that Mrs. Berry, moved to
a greater energy, as an irritated landlady,
knocked again. Soon after this, the door was
carefully opened, but only partly, just wide
enough for a man to show his face and one
side of his body.

'What have you done with my Tim?'
demanded Mrs. Higgins, immediately, recognising at once, by his white face and his
black clothes, the man who had seduced her
cat into his back room.

'What do you mean?' asked Mr. Blake,
softly, and very quietly. Mrs. Berry shivered,

for she thought there was something of a purr in the man's voice; and this reminded her, for the first time, that Mr. Blake's movements had always been soft and cat-like, and she was never sure whether her lodger was at home in his room or somewhere else.

'Mr. Blake,' began Mrs. Berry, recovering her firmness as a landlady, 'my friend, Mrs. Higgins, has seen you with her own eyes entice her cat into your room. If that is not so, you will not be afraid to let us come in and see for ourselves.'

'Certainly, ladies,' answered Mr. Blake, with the same pleasant purr. 'May I ask you to wait outside for a minute or two?'

With these words he closed the door, and the two women waited, exchanging looks, but passing no remarks.

Mr. Blake did not keep them waiting long, for in less than three minutes the door was again opened, and they were invited to enter, Mr. Blake saying that he would remain on the landing until they had finished their investigation.

This investigation did not take very long.
Mrs. Berry's first interest was to know how
her lodger lived in the way of food, and the
first thing she did was to open the door of a
small cupboard and glance over its contents.
The next moment she had raised the lid of a
saucepan, from which there came a strong,
pungent odour. It occurred to her now that
she had often smelt this before, and had
wondered what kind of meat her lodger
cooked, and whether it was really fit for
human consumption. This saucepan was
full of meat, and it looked something like
rabbit.

While this had been going on, Mrs. Higgins
had not been idle, for it was not very long
before she was holding up before Mrs.
Berry's horror-stricken eyes the skin of a
black cat! And the next moment Tim, dead
and cold, but unskinned, was lifted from
under the bed, while his mistress fell into a
chair and went off into a dead faint. Mrs.
Berry required no more evidence – William
Blake, her lodger, lived on boiled cat! The

disappearance of so many cats in the neighbourhood was no longer a mystery.

Mrs. Berry was not only a big, strong
woman physically, but she also had the
fighting spirit of a rough man. She was not
the gentle kind of creature that one would
choose to play snowballs with a fairy. This
being the case, it was not long before she was
making her way towards the landing, with
the intention of wringing Mr. Blake's neck,
and then throwing him into the gutter. But
she was too late for this, for when she reached
the landing it was only to find it unoccupied.
Mr. Blake, with his cat-like tread, had gone
down the stairs so silently that not one board
had creaked; and no one else could have done
this. He had realised that he was now a
condemned man, and it would have been only
waste of time if he had tried to hide the effects
of his work. So he thought it best to clear out
at once, and indulge his taste for boiled cat
in some other neighbourhood, letting Shore-
ditch, Deptford, Bethnal Green, or some other
Borough solve the meat problem for him.

He did not have the least hesitation in making up his mind to this, as he was leaving nothing of value behind him. For the room had been furnished by Mrs. Berry, and all it contained of his was a large empty box – which was brought to impress the landlady when he moved in – and a few dirty rags that were hardly worth washing, even with dog-soap.

That was the last of Mr. William Blake, as far as Lambeth was concerned. And now, if any one goes to Lambeth and inquires for the house where Blake had lived, it might save a lot of confusion if the inhabitants are told at once that the *poet* Blake is meant, and not the Blake who lived on boiled cat.

CHAPTER XI

THIS CHANGING LIFE

THE CUCKOO

When I was sitting near a stream,
 And watched the waves that came in
  turns
To butt the rocks that kept them in,
 Breaking their milk-white horns –
'Twas then a Cuckoo, full of joy,
 No man had seen in any place,
Perched on a tree before my eyes,
 And shouted in my face!

BIRDS do not like a windy day, and they
seldom sing when the wind is strong. Is it
because the wind deafens them and, their eyes
not having any support from their ears, makes
them think more of danger than of song?
But they like the rain, as much as I like it
myself. Whenever I walk in the rain, I always
sing or whistle. But the difference between a

bird and myself is this – that whereas I sing in the rain, a bird usually waits until it is over and he is wet through.

It is surprising to see how birds have adapted themselves to their surroundings, in the same way as cats and dogs. When I was a boy it was quite common to see dogs run over and killed by horses and carts. But in spite of the fast cars and lorries of the present day, it does not seem to me that more dogs are killed. The dogs have now become quicker and more alert, and have changed their character with the world's conditions. In the same way the birds still sing as much as ever, in spite of the noise of traffic. One time I used to think that the greatest objection to a flying-ship was that in sailing through the clouds it drove a Skylark down to earth, where it had no heart to sing. This is all wrong, for the Skylarks that centuries ago got their inspiration from silence, have now adapted themselves to the new conditions, and get their inspiration from the purr of a machine.

The Cuckoo should not, of course, be

introduced into a book on garden birds, seeing that he has a wandering spirit; and my only justification for doing so here is that one of these birds was hatched in my garden and reared under my very eyes. The nest was found as usual by my dog Betty, who had seen two little birds go in and out of a low hedge, and had sat up in front of it to draw my attention. So I approached at once and parted the leaves; and what I saw then took my breath away, and almost frightened me. For I saw a big baby bird in a very small nest, looking at me with large dark eyes. Seeing him there, filling the nest completely — making it difficult to see anything of the nest at all — filled me with astonishment, for I had no notion then of who or what he was. He was so big that his breast and wings over-lapped the nest and made a heavy rim of their own. Taking the dog in my arms, I stepped a safe distance back; and it was not long before I saw two little Robins enter the hedge, bringing food for a baby that was certainly not theirs. It then occurred to me for the first time that the strange bird was no other than a young Cuckoo.

Seeing that Cuckoo there, looking so tremendous and powerful because of his small setting, brought to mind several instances of where I had been fascinated by things that were much weaker than myself. I remembered one day when a woman brought me news that a mouse was under the stove. Although I expressed some surprise, I knew that my rooms were swarming with mice, but thought it wise to keep that knowledge to myself.

'There he is,' she whispered, pointing him out where he sat quietly under the stove, and eyeing us furtively. So we looked, and we looked; and as the mouse did not make the least move, we became fascinated at the sight. But all at once the woman gave a loud scream, which completely broke the spell. The mouse no sooner heard this than he disappeared, but I cannot say how or where. As I felt a little irritation, her scream being such a sudden shock to my nerves, I said at last, 'Why did you do that?'

'Because,' she answered calmly, 'I thought he was going to attack us!'

I remembered, too, the case of a very small boy, who was known as Bobby. On one occasion I saw this little mite, who was not much more than a baby, go up to a large sleeping dog and strike it across the face. The dog jumped up immediately and, showing its sharp teeth, prepared for battle. But the boy, having no fear or care, lifted his arm to strike again. Seeing this the dog, in fear of the child's indomitable spirit, turned around and slunk off. The doings of this child were always a fear and fascination, and I never passed him without speaking cheerfully, so as to make him respect my property. For it would have been impossible to kill this child's spirit, unless we killed his body, and no one could think of doing that.

I remembered how my neighbour next door caught this boy red-handed, picking the flowers in front of her house. How she had spoken to him kindly, and tried to extract a promise from him that he would not do it again. And how, failing to get an answer, she had threatened him with corporal punishment and, leading him to the gate, had pushed him roughly and forcibly away. But all through this ordeal, the child had never once blenched, nor had he uttered a word. Fortunately for this lady, she was not aware of what happened soon after. For I happened to be standing in my window, looking out, when I heard the click of my neighbour's gate, and saw Bobby about to enter. Wondering what the child was going to do, I watched, and it was not long before I was enlightened. For Bobby slowly and deliberately walked to the front door and piddled on my neighbour's doorstep! Any other boy, after doing this, would have hurried away, but this strange, indomitable child simply left as he came, with the same deliberation and unconcern. It will be understood from this that I left the lady and Bobby to their own affairs, and, for the sake of my own property, did nothing to interfere.

One day, when I was looking into a book,

I saw a picture of Bacchus as a child. Even
if I had not known the title, I would certainly
have known that I had before me the picture
of a young God. The majesty of the whole
thing, the curls on the head, the large eyes,
the round, firm lips, were convincing enough
– without seeing his chubby fist in the act of
crushing a bunch of grapes, with the knuckles
large and powerful. The tremendous impression made on me, when I saw this picture,
was never matched until this day, when I saw
a large baby Cuckoo spreading himself all
over a small nest, as a conqueror in placid
possession. And knowing how fascinated I
was myself at such a strange sight, I came to
the conclusion that the two small Robins were
in exactly the same predicament, and did not
feed it day and night because they loved or
pitied it, but were really mesmerised by the
bird's presence, and were under a spell that
destroyed their reason and common sense.
This large baby bird lying there so lordly,
in full possession of their nest, fascinated them
by his bold eyes, and then won their pity by

showing an empty mouth that demanded food to maintain its life. I arrived at this conclusion by a study of my own feelings. For the sight of that strange bird so fascinated me that I knew – if the two little Robins failed in their task and left it to starve – I myself would have visited it twenty times a day and fed it with my own hand. In fact, I would have been this Cuckoo's slave and constant attendant until it no longer needed my help. However, there was one thing to be said in favour of this young Cuckoo – that he departed at once, when strong enough, and did not expect any further assistance from his smaller friends. He did not linger in the garden, as a beggar, but left without even one cry of Cuckoo!

CHAPTER XII

AT NIGHT

OWLS

What music, Lord, these birds must feel,
　　That make no pleasant tune:
They fail by throat, yet in their hearts
　　How they enjoy the Moon!

When I sit thinking of my money,
　　Or lie in bed and snore –
'Te-who! Te-who!' they cry in wonder,
　　For the beauty at my door.

I HAVE always looked on the Owl's voice at
night as a friendly sound, although it sounds
rather weird and lonely. The reason I like
it so much is because it reminds me that I
am close to Nature; so that I can say to
myself, 'A country that's green and wild
enough for him, is wild enough and green
enough for me.' And that is why I enjoy the

Owl's voice at night as much as I enjoy the
Cuckoo's voice by day. Not only that, but
they both strike the same sweet note of
simplicity, with very little difference in their
cries. One cries 'Cuckoo!' the other cries
'Te-who!' while the human Baby, when
anything pleases it, can do no more than cry
'Ooh! Ooh!' which is the beginning and end
of all their wonder. And the whole three of
them, the Owl, Cuckoo, and Baby, are apt to
overdo it to the point of monotony, if nothing
interferes with their high spirits.

I believe I have said before that my knowledge of birds is not extensive, and that I
write more as a lover than a cold student.
But one night a certain man asked me such
a foolish question about birds that it almost
took my breath away. I had been attending
a small gathering of poetry-lovers, where
each member was expected to read a song,
poem, or lines on a given subject, the subject
of the night being 'On Birds.' My poem was
one by Thomas Heywood, while another
member read Keats' *Ode to a Nightingale*.

When the meeting was over, and we were going home, the reader of Keats and two others going my way – we were suddenly startled by hearing the wild screech of a passing bird. 'What bird was that?' asked one of the party, addressing me, because of my great love and interest in birds. I certainly did not know, but before I could make an answer, the admirer of Keats said quickly, 'Perhaps it is the Nightingale!' It seems that this man thought that any bird's voice heard at night must be the Nightingale's. And did he actually think that he had heard our sweetest bird singer, and that it could make a note like that, or did he have no ear for music? After reading Keats, too!

Near my house, at a corner facing west, we have a large pear tree that is not only rich in bearing fruit, but is also full of grace and beauty. Up to the present it has not lost a single bough, and there is no sign of decay in any part of it. It is so close to the house that some of the branches almost touch the maid's bedroom window.

But when I came down to breakfast this morning, the maid had a strange tale to tell, and all about this beautiful tree. For suddenly near midnight, she was wakened by the fierce beating of wings and the angry, excited cries of birds. She was so frightened at hearing this that she left her room and sat on the landing until the place became quiet. Being curious to know the meaning of this, I went forth at once to investigate, thinking to find some trace of this mystery. When I reached the tree, it occurred to me that two Thrushes had built their nest up towards the top. I remembered a day when my cat Pharaoh had climbed this tree, and how he had come down faster than he went up, being attacked fiercely by two birds. They had not only driven him to earth, but had even continued their attack until, running in fear of his life, he had reached the kitchen door, which, luckily for him, happened to stand wide open. I had seen all this with my own eyes, and now looked for the nest, thinking that the mystery was centred there. And I was quite right in this, for I now saw that the nest was not only turned on its side but was also fallen to a lower branch. It was quite obvious that the nest had been attacked by larger birds, either Magpies or Owls, and that the two parent Thrushes had beat them back time after time, until their strength was gone altogether. Their young ones had been murdered, in spite of the spirited defence of their parents, and the bodies dragged out of the nest and carried away. If I wanted proof of this I saw it in the upturned nest. For further proof I saw two Thrushes standing near it, looking at each other in a kind of stupor, as though they did not know where to go or what to do next. However, the poor things recovered after a while, and went away, probably to start a new life in a new place. I was glad of this, for I began to think that if they remained there much longer, in that state of depression, I would have to be cruel to be kind and force them to leave; which would have had the double effect of relieving both their feelings and my own.

But it must not be thought that while this maid was having such a bad night, that I myself was lying quietly in bed and sleeping well. Early in the night I had heard an Owl, and this bird's voice had given me the usual pleasure. But, unfortunately, the cry of this particular bird had given pain to a wandering dog, who had sat outside my house indulging in the most pitiful howls, which frightened the Owl away. And then, to make matters worse, an old neighbour, who was crazy at times, had one of her worst fits and with her windows wide open began to damn the whole world, and all it contained. The effect of this woman's voice was to frighten the howling dog, even as the dog had frightened the Owl — and the old woman was then left to carry on in silence. The great trouble was that I lived near enough to hear her words, and curiosity kept me awake, even when her voice went low. This woman always started in the same way, crying out in a high, shrill voice, 'I have paid for my bread, and I have paid for my meat. I have paid for my lodgings.

Whoever says that I have not done these things are liars and only fit for burning in hell!'

This poor woman's fit of abuse usually lasted fifteen or twenty minutes, and her voice could be heard all over the neighbourhood. Her idea was to keep her windows wide open, day and night, so that she could walk her rooms at any time and shoo the devils out. She also kept a light burning at all hours, to keep evil spirits away. It was probably owing to the latter, that she carried this light about at night, from attic to cellar, and endangered property and the lives of other human beings – that people were at last successful in getting her removed to another place, where she would be forcibly restrained. But although I suffered more than others, who lived farther away, I made no complaint to get rid of her, in spite of being asked and encouraged to do so.

She has now been taken away, and I am left with a clean conscience that I did nothing against her, either in word or deed. But I

must say that the experience was weird and
uncanny, to hear that mad woman's voice
rising in force in the middle of the night.
The only thing I ever said against her was
when I was asked by some one in authority if
her language was foul. To this I answered
simply, more than once, 'Her language was
picturesque.'

OLD AND CRAZY

Though rising early with the Lark –
How can she sing, whose mind is dark!
She burns her lamp by night and day,
To keep the evil spirits away;
With windows opened wide at night,
She puts the lurking devils to flight.

How many nights have heard her wrath,
That cursed all things in Heaven and Earth!
Till, tired of all her terrible speech,
Only the Owl was left to screech.
When children wake and, trembling, cry –
Who blames the poor old Owl? Not I.